Caffeinate
Your Career

Career Management One Cup at a Time

by Jennifer Way

THINK·DO
media

Caffeinate Your Career by Jennifer Way

Text and Design © 2017 Jennifer Way

ThinkDo Media
615 Main Street
Suite 201
Nashville, TN 37206

Ordering Information: Quantity sales and orders by U.S. trade bookstores and wholesalers. Special discounts are available on quantity purchases by corporations, associations, and others. For details, contact the publisher at the address above.

The ThinkDo Media name and the TDM emblem are trademarks of ThinkDo Media.

Visit the book website at caffeinateyourcareer.com.
Visit the author's website at jenniferwayspeaks.com

First Edition.

ISBN 978-0-9977597-0-9

First Printing: April 2017

14 13 12 11 10 / 10 9 8 7 6 5 4 3 2 1

CONTENTS

YOUR COMMITMENT TO COFFEE

What's your favorite morning drink? Are you a coffee drinker? A tea person? A soda person, perhaps? Morning caffeine is a ritual for many people. I'm a fruit tea kinda girl myself. Regardless of position or title, we don't miss out on our morning caffeine.

The coffee industry knows this. It doesn't matter if you're running late, you'll still stop for coffee. We provide coffee at nearly every meeting. We even have specific meetings around coffee. We guard our morning caffeine religiously. "Don't talk to me until I've had my coffee" is a phrase I've heard often around the office. Some people need a second cup before they begin to interact.

Few people have the same vigor for managing their careers as they do for their morning caffeine. Most people fear that career management is hard or takes a tremendous amount of time. This book is my answer to that.

My purpose is to help people highlight and value their skills and abilities and express them through their work. It's why I'm on the earth. Career management can be a simple ritual that we incorporate into what we're already doing. It's the caffeine for our career. Hence, *Caffeinate Your Career* was born.

This is about adding that little boost of energy into your daily work routine that will serve you long into the future. It doesn't mean more work; we just have to prioritize career management more. We certainly prioritize our morning coffee.

But who has the time, right? What if you could wake up and shake up your career in 15 minutes a day or less? This book is a collection of easy actions that require very little time. In fact, you won't find any wild and crazy ideas that no one else has thought of. No, this book is designed to help you become intentional and mindful of actions that will quickly and easily change the trajectory of your career — all in 15 minute increments. Caffeinate Your Career is about simple, small activities you can do in less time than it takes to finish your morning coffee.

Wouldn't it be great if you got tapped on the shoulder for your next role, or better yet they designed a role around what you wanted to do? Do you wish you had access to resources that your current company doesn't provide? Do you dream of doing more than fake work that never seems to amount to anything? All of this is possible if you take the wheel and fuel your career.

Work these actions into your daily schedule and you'll have the keys to unlock better work assignments, more money, and greater opportunities.

If you want your career to fuel you then you have to take time to fuel your career. It's simple. It may not always be easy, but it is definitely simple. Let's get started.

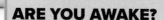

1

ARE YOU AWAKE?

Maybe you are super
motivated and looking
for your next big
project. Maybe you've

been asleep at the wheel and suffered some ill effects. No matter how well intended, it's easy to let your to-do list overwhelm managing your own career. We get so wrapped up in daily tasks that we forget what it takes to have a thriving career. That's what I mean when I say that so many have fallen asleep.

I know... we're just too busy. We tell ourselves that it's not a priority. We have to focus on what we get paid to do. This is half true, but the part we forget is that our career is at stake. We don't have to be this tired. There are simple things we can do every day that will make a real difference.

This book is about waking up your career and making sure you never fall into a "career coma." This is about getting unstuck, ending our boredom, and reviving the sense of challenge and fulfillment that all of us long for from our work.

This is about winning the best work assignments and promotions. This is about creating vitality in our work. This is about owning your career. You are the boss of you. No one can do it for you; not your boss, not your company, and not your mama. Only *you* have the power to change your work. Will you seize it?

Taking Your Temperature: Assessing Your Career Health

There are ten areas that contribute to the health and well-being of any career:

1. Quality of Work
2. Relationship with Leadership
3. Relationship with Team
4. Professional Presence & Communication
5. Learning and Growth
6. Network Activity
7. Industry Contribution & Recognition
8. Career Champions
9. Recognition and Rewards
10. Career Planning

If you begin to take small and easy steps in each of these areas, there's no telling where your career will take you.

Let's get to work!

2

TAKE YOUR TEMPERATURE

Take a few minutes and assess your career for yourself. If you don't have a solid idea of where you are, it will be hard to feel like you're making any progress or realize where you can go.

Everyone has areas of managing their career that come more naturally than others. The following is an assessment that highlights areas where your career is strong, as well as areas where you might be vulnerable. That's the key; isn't it? You should be making conscious choices about where to concentrate your efforts for the type of rewards you seek, but also to ensure your well-being in case something happens to your job, company, or industry.

Position yourself to come out ahead no matter what. You can fool-proof your career. You can boss-proof it, economy-proof it, and actually thrive in spite of all the things you can't control. Wake up and take control of the things you can.

Take fifteen minutes and complete this assessment. Use the results to skip around from chapter to chapter for specific exercises. Or plow through the book from start to finish. It's up to you how you want to use it.

OPPORTUNITIES ARE USUALLY DISGUISED AS HARD WORK, SO MOST PEOPLE DON'T RECOGNIZE THEM.

- ANN LANDERS

15 MINUTES

CAREER ASSESSMENT

The following assessment is a collection of questions relating to career health and "awakeness." Rate each question on a scale of 1 to 10, where 1 is low and 10 is high.

1. How would you rate the quality of your work assignments? Think about this in terms of how happy are you with the type of assignments you receive and the visibility of those assignments.

2. How would you rate the quality of the relationship you have with leadership? This could include both your manager and executive leaders in your organization.

3. How well do you present yourself? Does your appearance match the career goals you aspire to? Think about how your professional presence and communication compares to others who are successful in similar roles.

4. Rate the quality of the relationship you have with peers and those who report to you. Think about the level of trust and respect you share.

RATE **5.** How would you rate your learning and growth at this point in your career? Are you learning now? When was the last time you learned a new skill? Think about how you are stretching in or outside your current role.

RATE **6.** How active are you with your network? Think about how much value you are offering or receiving from your network.

RATE **7.** Rate your contribution to your industry. How are you recognized for that contribution?

RATE **8.** How would you rate your ability to identify and cultivate relationships with your career champions? Think about how intentional you are with people who will advocate for you in your role and in your career.

RATE **9.** Rate how you are rewarded and recognized for your work results. This should include salary and other compensation and perhaps things like flexibility, access to learning opportunities, awards, and more.

RATE **10.** How proactive have you been about planning your career? Think about how you have achieved next steps in your career over time. Was it by plan or more by chance?

HOW TO INTERPRET THIS ASSESSMENT

Change is inevitable. This assessment is less about your current role and more about the overall health of your career. Awakeness is about being proactive. What are the behaviors and steps you can take to make an impact in any of these areas? Look for opportunities for you to reduce your risk and gage how vulnerable you might be should things change unexpectedly.

DAY OLD COFFEE
**Highly Vulnerable -
Focus on Resilience**

It is likely that if something were to happen to your current role, you may be forced to change your lifestyle. Most people are too wrapped up in their current role.

It's hard for people in this situation to be resilient as they are out of touch with the market. Most are very surprised at how difficult it is to replace their title, money, and status in a new role.

Address any areas where your skills might have grown stale. Focus on industry trends and updating your skills to reduce the risk and impact to your lifestyle.

50-59 POINTS

INSTANT COFFEE

Vulnerable -
Lifestyle Impact

You are handing the control in your career to others. Any change in your current situation would impact your lifestyle. People in this category might miss the signals that changes are on the horizon and be caught off guard. Folks in this category are often blind to very real opportunities that surround them. Don't wait for something to happen before you take action. Focus on easy changes that don't require extensive effort to greatly increase the stability of your career. Get involved in a professional association or skill building activities to start.

60-69

GAS STATION COFFEE

Passive -
Recognize Opportunity

Your career is on cruise control. People in this category might recognize opportunities and might even want access to an opportunity, but they are often invisible to those who have the power to grant an opportunity.

Focus on increasing access to those with influence and increasing your visibility. People need to know more about how to value and reward your contributions.

OFFICE COFFEE

Active -
Tapped for Opportunity

Not only do you recognize opportunities, you are in pursuit of them. You are known and recognized in your organization and often consulted for your opinion. Your hard work is rewarded.

Focus on being more visible in your industry and learn how to effectively advertise your wins and you will find people tap you for opportunities you couldn't even know are out there.

80+

POINTS

ARTISAN COFFEE

Resilient -
Creating Opportunities

You are very resilient to any market shifts or changes in your work environment. You likely see what's coming down the pike and position yourself to take advantage of what might be coming. You are likely perceived as a thought leader.

Focus on influencing your industry. Find ways to increase your influence by leading others. Lead inside and outside of your industry. Continue to learn from other industries and apply those lessons in a new way to your industry.

3

QUALITY OF WORK

What you actually do on a day by day basis has a huge impact on how you feel about your

work, and how you feel about it effects the quality. Think about the tasks you perform every day and skills you use to complete them. Are you assigned the best projects to work on? Do you feel challenged without being overwhelmed?

A Gallup Study suggests that having autonomy, or the power of self-direction, has a large impact on how satisfied you are with your work. How your work fits with your team and with your company as a whole impacts the quality, too.

Here are some exercises that will improve the quality of your work.

5 MINUTES

Focus on achievements.

Keep a list of all of your accomplishments today. Avoid that feeling that you didn't accomplish anything by tracking all of the projects you're working on. Maybe you start by listing your completed tasks, but don't stop there. Ask yourself why that task matters.

Typically, if you ask that three times, you'll find the value that you're really creating. This will help you communicate with others about the value you bring every day.

5 MINUTES

Lead with your service and ask for what you need.

The next time you're asked to do something or turn something in, respond with, "I'm happy to do that (*service*), and what I'll need is…. (*resources*)." Fill in the blanks for your work. Using this strategy will help you get access to the resources you need to produce a quality work product.

ACTION

Find three things you can delegate to someone else today. Odds are, you shouldn't be doing this work in the first place. Who should or could do this work? Who could use this work as a learning opportunity? How can you successfully move this list off your plate?

10 MINUTES

Learn from a top producer.

Think about who you know that does high quality work. What makes their work product stand out? What can you learn from them? Book a meeting with them and share your observations about their work product. Ask their advice on a specific project and what they might recommend to improve it.

10 MINUTES

Brainstorm.

Brainstorm for ten minutes on what resources would make your job easier. Is there another department that has this resource? Can you borrow it? Rent it? Outsource it? Think about a creative way to get access to that resource and focus on improving your results.

10 MINUTES

Contemplate high quality vs. perfectionism.

Think about the difference between high quality and perfectionism. How can you tell the difference? Is 80% good enough? What's enough? Don't let perfectionism rob you of your effectiveness.

10 MINUTES

ACTION

Take ten minutes and clear one desk surface. Set a timer and recycle the paper, get rid of the sticky notes, and sort out the piles. Don't just stash it in the credenza! Address your mess—it's only ten minutes.

15 MINUTES

Create templates. Place them in a "template" folder in your email program.

Pull some of your best emails, those you use most often, and place them in a folder for the next time you need one. Templates allow you the opportunity for high quality communication, and they improve the quality of how you talk about your work.

15 MINUTES

Think about today's top priority.

How could you improve the quality of your deliverable? Is it well-organized? Does it require further definition? Will others find it clear and complete? Could some visual design improve the level of clarity? Would you be happy, or embarrassed, if your boss showed it to your CEO?

15 MINUTES

Find or create an inspiring project.

If you're not inspired by any of your current projects, what is something you could work on that would bring value without taking resources away from your current work? Who could you brainstorm with to help you figure out something that would inspire you?

4

LEADERSHIP FRIENDLY

Leaders have an incredible amount of influence on our future. Neglecting to build

relationships with key leaders isn't about avoiding "brown-nosing." It's limiting your own future.

Look for small ways to genuinely connect and bring value to leaders. Ask yourself what your leaders find attractive, and then follow through and show your value. Are they interested in achievement? Do they value feeling like a teacher? Do they value innovation or efficiency? Look to connect with their professional interests. It doesn't hurt for them to like you. You will need their support for ANY good thing to happen in your near future.

5 MINUTES

Ask someone to share your value.

Find opportunities to share the value that you're providing--better yet, get someone to share that on your behalf. The next time someone has a positive comment about your work, simply ask them to write that down and email your boss with it. Keep it light and positive, but remind people to sing your praises for you.

ACTION

Determine what your boss' preferred communication methods are. Do they favor in-person, instant message, phone, or email? What time of day or day of the week is best to approach him or her? When would your boss prefer to be included in your communication? What's too much coomunication for your boss?

5 MINUTES

Identify what your boss values.

What does your boss value most? Accomplishment, the "big picture," process, people? Think about what question they consistently lead with first. Then, mirror that when you communicate back to them. Is it about people? Tasks? Process? The "big picture?" Avoid the tendency to lead with what *you* think is important. Gain their attention by leading with what *they* think is important. If you can't tell, start with the "big picture" and limit the details you share.

15 MINUTES

Design your dream role.

In fifteen minutes, brainstorm about the role you want next. What are the skills and resources you would require for such a role? Can you design a role around an opportunity, which maybe only you can see at this point? What is the business case for a role like this? Toss it around, and if it holds water, pitch the idea to your boss.

10 MINUTES

ACTION

Take ten minutes and thank your boss for something they've done to help you professionally. Simple acknowledgement is a powerful motivator. Reward the positive behavior if you want more of it. Determine if email, a handwritten note, or a verbal acknowledgement is best.

15 MINUTES

Share an article that's on trend.

Spend fifteen minutes online, and find a relevant article or blog post to share with your boss or a couple of influential leaders. Try to make it something noteworthy or connected to what you're working on. Use Google for recent statistics, trends, or provocative industry news. Use other social media outlets like Twitter or LinkedIn to bring this information to attention.

15 MINUTES

Find a solution.

Think about something that isn't working in your department or current position. Brainstorm for fifteen minutes about possible solutions. Don't edit yourself. Make a list of solutions. Pick the best solution, and carefully talk to your boss about it. Focus on the solution and don't dwell too much on the problem. You want to be viewed as a problem-solver and not a complainer.

15 MINUTES

List your boss's top three priorities.

Guess what your boss' priorities are at the moment. List them out. Include some ways that you can assist or demonstrate your commitment to the boss' priorities? Then, ask your boss to confirm their top three priorities. Share the best ideas from your list about how you can provide support.

5

PROFESSIONAL PRESENCE & COMMUNICATION

In fancy coffee shops, how they present a coffee is a big deal. The color, the whipped crème and even the images they create in the coffee are all a part of the experience.

How you present yourself matters, too. Creating a strong presence will inspire others to have confidence in you and your ability to do your work. If you don't look the part, you won't get the part. This includes how you dress, to what degree you follow trends; haircut, glasses, jewelry, and even shoes. Think of this like buying the right tools. You might be able to do the job without the right tools, but it sure does work to your advantage if you have them.

Outdated looks or details communicate poor skills or being out of touch with current market trends. Communicate a proactive work style and set people up to cooperate with what you are trying to achieve. Invest in your tools. Here are a few ideas to inspire your professional presence.

5 MINUTES

Redesign a subject line to drive action.

Revise one subject line in your email to clearly reflect the correct topic and urgency of your message. For example, "Insurance Claim Due Friday at 3pm" or "Your Input on Project X,Y,Z is Requested," instead of a generic subject line. People are busy. Set up your communication so that it moves people to do what you need them to do.

5 MINUTES

Name your three differentiators.

What are three things that define you professionally and make you different than others with your job title? Use these criteria to prioritize your projects and determine what new projects you should pursue. Look for opportunities to reinforce these things in your daily work activities.

5 MINUTES

Organize your communication into templates.

Make a list of all the types of communications you frequently send. How many templates would you need in order to cut back the emails you have to write? Make a list of templates that would be helpful. For example, a LinkedIn invitation response, meeting follow-up, a thanks for a first meeting, and more.

ACTION

Whether "inbox zero" is a possibility for you or not, set a timer for ten minutes and clear as many emails from your account as possible. Clear out the junk and consider unsubscribing from newsletters you don't actually read.

10 MINUTES

Inform? Request? Or clarify?

Analyze one email you are about to send. Determine the purpose for your email. Are you informing someone of something, asking for something, or confirming information? Understanding your goal, and stating it clearly up front, will help people understand your expectations and what you need from them.

15 MINUTES

ACTION

Find one blog post on how to run a productive meeting. Read the article. Write an agenda for your next meeting.

15 MINUTES

Evaluate successful images.

Take a look at the people in positions that you want. How do they dress? What kind of haircut, jewelry, or accessories do they wear? How similar or differently do you dress? Maybe it's time for a bit of a makeover. Name one action you could take this week to strengthen your professional image.

15
MINUTES

ACTION

Spend fifteen minutes and clean up your computer files. Getting organized will help you be more efficient. You can save yourself a tremendous amount of time by gaining easy access to the information you need. It sends a powerful message of competency when you are organized.

15 MINUTES

ACTION

Read a blog post on the latest trend in presentation skills. What should you change or update in the way that you present? Is it about graphic design? Lessening the content on each slide? What's going to effectively translate your message to your audience? Consider joining a toastmaster's club for practice.

6

RELATIONSHIP WITH TEAM

Your team is directly responsible for your success. Your work life is *so* much better or *so*

much worse due to your relationships with co-workers. A large portion of your overall success depends on the quality of relationships you cultivate with key co-workers.

Familiarity can cause us to make assumptions about how our co-workers experience us. Each of the following actions offer an opportunity to be deliberate with your co-workers. Taking time to build a strong relationship with your peers, and those who work for you, is the right thing to do as a human being, but it's also in your own best interest.

5 MINUTES

Improve your follow-up.

Follow up three times in two ways before you give up. Who are you waiting for a response from at this moment? Who owes you a call or email? Identify their communication preference. Do they prefer phone, email, or do you need to hang out by their desk? If you're the one who needs something, it's your job to be the one to pursue it.

5 MINUTES

Acknowledge a team member's success.

Write an email to your team member (and copy your boss) to acknowledge their specific contribution. What actions did you observe them perform? How did that affect the overall success of the project? Document the acknowledgement and share it with key stakeholders.

ACTION

Look for a recent statistic, which is relevant to what you're working on, and introduce it to your colleagues. Use Google Scholar, LinkedIn, or other social media platforms to identify and find the statistic. Glance at what your competition is publishing. There may be some useful competitive analysis you could utilize.

10 MINUTES

Evaluate your boundaries.

Think about the emotional boundaries you have with your peers or team members at work. Remember they will always be your colleague, before they are your friend. Assess your relationships. Are there any that you need to renegotiate in order to keep the personal and professional line clear?

ACTION

Identify one ex-colleague, whom you haven't spoken with for a year, and give them a call or an email. Ask them what they are working on and how you can help them. Feel free to share a bit about what you're doing as well, but make sure to focus on how you can support *them* or bring *them* value.

15 MINUTES

How would your co-workers describe your work?

Create a list of the people you work with regularly. Beside their names, write down how you think *they* would describe your work. What could you do to improve or change it? What is evidence that they might feel this way? How do you know?

15

ACTION

What are the communication preferences of your teammates? List the team members you work with, and what you think *their* preferences are. Are they morning people or afternoon people? Do they prefer email, phone calls, instant messaging or in-person talk? Once you've thought about it and made your list, ask several people on the list.

15 MINUTES

Negotiate for uninterrupted work time.

Find one way to increase your productive work time. Think about your work culture. Is it okay to shut your door and turn off your phone? How can you gain more uninterrupted work time? Is there a way to negotiate with a colleague to answer interruptions on a set schedule and then trade so you can both get some uninterrupted work time? Blocking time on your calendar for focus is essential for creating anything new.

15 MINUTES

Birthday wishes.

Create a calendar of your team members' birthdays and work anniversaries. Do it at one time, so you can pre-program calendar reminders for yourself. Make sure you acknowledge everyone's special day. Create a pre-programmed email and schedule it, if you need assistance to remember.

7

LEARNING AND GROWTH

Continual improvement is a basic component of a successful business. It's essential to ensuring

your success, too.

Diving into new skill-sets, or honing a specific skill, is key to evolving over time in your career. It's not always practical, or even necessary, to sign up for a new class or to go back to college for a degree. Realistically, with your current schedule, what are you doing to improve yourself? To develop or improve a skill? Be mindful and deliberate in your improvement. Here are a few suggestions...

ACTION

What educational benefits does your current employer provide? Think beyond tuition reimbursement. Do they have a conference budget? Do they offer access to online tutorials? What's one thing you can do to take advantage of this benefit?

10 MINUTES

Volunteer for an event.

Find an educational opportunity such as an event, conference, or meeting with a speaker. Volunteer to work it. Send an email to the conference manager.

Maybe they'll let you attend for free. Focus on expanding your network and your skills. You never know who you will meet or how it might lead to other opportunities or resources. You might even meet the next person you will hire.

10 MINUTES

Leverage a skill superstar.

Name one skill that you feel you lack, or in which you feel weak. Whose superpower is this skill? Who do you know that could point you to a person with mastery in this skill? See if you can book them for lunch and get some pointers to improve in a particular skill.

10 MINUTES

Industry trends.

What is one new area your industry is moving toward? What is one thing you can incorporate to add this new skill? Is there a meet-up on the topic? Who can you talk to about this? Don't overlook connections outside your organization.

ACTION

Who is the most technically savvy of your co-workers? Take fifteen minutes and ask them to give you their best tech tip to make you more efficient. Is it a keyboard shortcut? A new app? Some way to automate a task? Adopt tips related to what you do all the time. Bit by bit, these actions save a lot of time.

15 MINUTES

Learn from your competition.

Who are your company's direct competitors? Who do you know that works at any of those companies? Follow them on social media, and see what they're talking about. Check out their thought leaders and what they are publishing.

15 MINUTES

ACTION

Play around with Google Scholar. It indexes a wide variety of research and studies. Review for insight related to your industry or for content applicable to your work and daily deliverables.

15 MINUTES

Research online education.

Check out free university online lectures or classes. Spend fifteen minutes searching Lynda, Udemy, or other online classes to see what might be relevant to your daily work life.

Online courses which incur a cost might even be covered or reimbursed by your current employer.

8

COFFEE TALK: NETWORK ACTIVITY

I don't know too many people who really have time to go to coffee in the middle of their day.

Networking should go far beyond an invite that may even be inconvenient to accept.

Few people claim to love networking, but it may be the most powerful way to advance your career. Think about it: almost all good things that happen to you in your career come from someone you know. We think of this when it comes to finding a new job, but it's how you might find the next person you're going to hire or work with, how you might find out about a new tool or resource, and so much more.

Networking is about growing meaningful relationships *intentionally*. This is not about using and abusing people. It's about finding connections and reaching out with thoughtful and genuine effort in consistent and natural ways.

If you do that, you will grow real and powerful relationships.

You don't have to be an extrovert, or attend a million after-hours events. There are all kinds of ways to foster a strong network. Here are just a few exercises to support you.

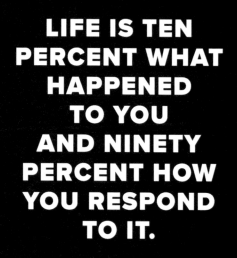

LIFE IS TEN PERCENT WHAT HAPPENED TO YOU AND NINETY PERCENT HOW YOU RESPOND TO IT.

- LOU HOLTZ

5 MINUTES

Preview the guest list.

Look at the guest list for the next professional event you are planning to attend. Find three people on the list, which you would like to meet. Look them up on LinkedIn to familiarize yourself with their background, what they are talking about on social media, and connect with them.

ACTION

Find a relevant online resource and send it to three people in your network. This could be an article, a website, a study—whatever you've recently found valuable, or that you think *they* would view as valuable. Ask for feedback to refine what you share in the future.

5 MINUTES

Invite someone to an event.

Find a professional event that has an interesting topic. Invite someone who has grown stale in your network, or someone who could be particularly valuable to your network, to attend with you.

5 MINUTES

Mimic big connectors.

Who are the three most connected people you know? What business events are they going to in the next two weeks? Email them and ask if you can tag along. Watch how they network and how they work the room. Create an opportunity to observe them and learn whether they are conscious of it or not.

10 MINUTES

ACTION

Write a thank you note to someone who has recently helped you in some way. Hand-written notes are amazing. Don't let excuses — like a lack or postage, or a lack of fancy cards — stand in the way. Just do it!

10 MINUTES

Set a goal for the next event.

Spend ten minutes and define a goal or two for your next networking event. What do you want? What will you offer? Remember, this can be an event inside your organization or even outside of your industry.

10 MINUTES

Identify the holes in your network.

Spend ten minutes thinking about what your network is lacking. Is it a specific skill set? Is it a level of experience? Where could you go to find this? Who is most likely to have it as a part of their network? Who could you ask?

ACTION

Find one blog article on how to start a conversation or small talk with a stranger. This will come in handy the next time you are in a situation and need to be able to create a quick connection. You never know where a random conversation will lead.

10 MINUTES

Identify outside professionals.

Make a list of ten professionals outside of your organization that you respect. Put a note in your calendar to call and ask three of them to coffee, one per month over the next three months.

10 MINUTES

First meeting email template.

Take ten minutes and write an introductory template email to use the next time you meet someone for the first time. What information should you include? Do you want to invite them to connect on social media? Give yourself a chance to think about it *before* you need to send it.

15

ACTION

Spend fifteen minutes making a list
of how you can bring others value. Is
it an introduction to someone? Can
you offer a tech tip? Refer them to a
resource? Listing how you can bring
value will make it easier to identify
the next opportunity you have to do
so.

15 MINUTES

Backup your network.

Your contacts are the lifeblood of your career. Take a few minutes and back up your contacts so you have them ready and available to you outside the office.

ACTION

You don't have to be a graphic designer to make a business card. Go to Moo.com or Vistaprint and look at their designs. Create one for yourself. Consider including your name, brand statement or specialty, cell phone, and email address. Save the design and ask a couple people to review it. When you've got what you want, print them up!

9

INDUSTRY CONTRIBUTION & RECOGNITION

In order for professional opportunities to find you, you have to be known, inside and

outside of your industry, for your skills. This sounds pretty basic, but people gloss over this regularly. It starts with the skills you have to offer. If you're not clearly communicating what you've been working on to those in your industry, they won't think to call you the next time the need for those skills arises.

There are fast and easy ways to do this. Figuring out who you are is where it all starts.

ACTION

Research one professional association that's related to your field. Find out when their next meeting is scheduled. Sign up and put it on your calendar to attend.

5 MINUTES

Ask for good programming.

Make a list of talks you would enjoy attending, and which would contribute to your industry. Ask the head of programming to review your list.

ACTION

Pick a contact, in another part of your industry, and craft a recommendation for their LinkedIn page. Post it. Then, ask them for the same.

10 MINUTES

Post-event speaker acknowledgement.

After you attend an industry event, pick one speaker or moderator and write them an email acknowledging something specific which you learned or appreciated about their presentation. Bonus points if you share your supportive opinion on social media!

10 MINUTES

Volunteer for an event-based task for your professional organization.

Call up the board member in charge of volunteering, and introduce yourself. Volunteer in some small way in a relevant professional association. Can you send out a mailer? Greet new members? Work the sign-in desk? Being active sends a strong message about the quality of professional you really are.

ACTION

Write a thank you note to someone in your industry from whom you have learned, recently. Be specific about what you learned within the note and ask how you can reciprocate.

10 MINUTES

Create a shared media experience.

Win more exposure by partnering with a service that goes hand-in-hand with your own. Create an opportunity for cross-promotion.

Write an email to your contact, and ask to interview them for your newsletter, conference, or social media page. Offer to do the same with them.

Mutual complementary exposure is always a plus!

15 MINUTES

Showcase your skills.

Find one non-profit and call them to see if you can volunteer in a way that is related to your profession. Are you trying to become a manager? Take a board role for your professional association. Are you an accountant? Offer to do the bookkeeping for a charity that's important to you. Let people, other than your co-workers, see you in action. If you're trying to break into a new career, this is an excellent way to gain work experience.

15 MINUTES

Introduce yourself to a board member.

Who is on the board of your favorite professional association? Research them on LinkedIn to learn about their background and professional history. Reach out to one or two of them and introduce yourself. Find out a bit more about them and share a bit about your experience. You never know when that connection will lead to your next career move.

15 MINUTES

Outline an article for your industry or professional association newsletter.

Pick an industry relevant topic that would be interesting, practical, and actionable for others in your association. Outline three major points that you would include in the article as well as a followup action item or additional resource. Now put this in an email and pitch it to the head of communications and see how they respond to your idea. Whether they want you to work up the article or not is almost beside the point. You want to be viewed as a contributor.

10

CAREER CHAMPIONS

The idea of a career
champion is foreign to a
lot of people. A career
champion is someone

who will **proactively advocate** for you in your career. A champion could be inside or outside of your organization. They could even be inside or outside your industry, though typically it's more powerful to be in the same or complementary industries.

Your relationship with them could be short-term or long-term and they may not even be conscious you've designated them as someone you'd like to be an advocate. Think of these people as your career PR folks. The trick is figuring out who would make a great champion and why it's not only in your interest, but in **their** interest, to advocate for you.

Benevolence is a great reason for someone to champion for you, but it's more likely that you give someone a reason to advocate for you. Here are a few actions that might lead to cultivating your champions.

5 MINUTES

Become an influencer.

Who is one person that you could help grow professionally inside your organization? Look for one opportunity to help them today.

5 MINUTES

Go with a champion.

Invite a career champion to attend an event with you or wrangle an invitation to attend one with them. Bonding time during the commute, lunch, or break times can be invaluable. The key is to be ready to share important updates and build a greater relationship at every opportunity.

ACTION

What introduction do you think is important for your future? Who should know about you and the quality of your work? Who could offer a worthy introduction?

5 MINUTES

Ask for career advice.

Pick one internal career champion and get advice on the next steps in your career. Make it casual, but intentional. What areas should you consider? Where do they think the next opportunity might come from within the organization? Who's likely to make decisions on this type of opportunity?

5 MINUTES

Make your champion a recipient.

Champions are always asked for information or for actions that benefit a recipient. This time, make your champion a recipient. Ask a champion how you can bring them value. Could you offer to make an introduction? Help them with a technology issue? Identify a tool or resource that might be helpful? Don't make it weird. Stick to being professional and don't go overboard.

10 MINUTES

Champion someone else.

Who do you champion for in their career? What qualities make that person a good choice? Who you support is a strong reflection on yourself. Be cautious about who you are tied to. Get vocal about your support.

ACTION

Write a thank you note that specifically outlines how a champion has helped you. Bring them a coffee or include a gift card for a coffee. You can do it right online. You don't even have to go to the coffee shop to buy it.

15 MINUTES

Assess your relationship with potential influencers.

Who are the top three most influential people to your future in your organization? List their names, titles, and why you think they will be influencers. Now rank their level of support for you. Are they an advocate? Supportive? Neutral? How much influence will they likely have? High? Medium? Or low? What do you need to do now that you've thought about it?

15 MINUTES

Define your message.

Name three things you wish your career champions knew about how you work. What is the best way to communicate that to them? Can someone communicate this on your behalf? Which approach is better?

15 MINUTES

Determine an industry champion.

Who is someone, outside of your company, who could champion you inside of your industry? Book a lunch or coffee with them. Ask their advice on your career trajectory. What new skills should you be acquiring? What is their assessment of the market?

11

RECOGNITION & REWARDS

Almost everyone thinks
about salary when they
think about recognition
or rewards, and salary

is important. But it's about so much more than just money. Do you have more flexibility than your co-workers? Are you rewarded with better work assignments or more visibility?

In order to know you're valued, evaluate another opportunity, or even to decide if you should consider another opportunity; you have to first remember all the ways you're already being recognized.

Day-to-day work life makes it hard to remember what you may take for granted. You can be a lot happier if you remember all the things that are working for you now—not just what you're missing.

It's only after you evaluate your situation objectively and review **all** of the ways you're recognized and rewarded in your current position that can you figure out where the opportunity for more recognition or rewards might lie.

ACTION

Search online for a salary calculator and look up your job title in your geography. Find out how much others in your position, and your part of the country, are making. That will help you gauge where you are on the scale. It's hard to know how you are being rewarded, if you're not aware of market shifts outside your organization.

5 MINUTES

Big win reminder.

Look at your calendar and estimate when a project, where you're doing well, will wrap up. Then, set a reminder a couple weeks ahead of that to have a conversation with your boss about the project. When things are going well, after you've had a big win or a positive review, ask your boss specifically what it would take for you to get a raise or win a promotion. Ask them if they will partner with you to make that happen.

ACTION

Identify one person who is doing an excellent job. Write them a thank you email and name specific observations about what they've done well. Good things come to people who are good to others.

5 MINUTES

Reward yourself.

Shop online and pick out one "luxury" item. Using this as a reward, what is one goal you could set to achieve, which would make you feel as though you earned that luxury? Set up a savings plan and feed it $5 at a time — you know, the price of a coffee, to save for your item.

ACTION

Identify how you are contributing to your industry. Would it be beneficial to share that with your boss or team members? Be thoughtful about this. It has to align with your boss' values, or it could be used against you. Does it make your boss look good? Does it represent your company? Does it align with what your boss wants you to work on? If yes, then share. If not, keep it to yourself.

10 MINUTES

Assess boss behaviors.

Think about how your boss rewards and recognizes great performance. Is it prime work assignments, promotions, raises, public acknowledgement? What does your boss value most? Accomplishment? Being low-maintenance? Good judgment? Relationships outside the department?

10 MINUTES

Remember the value you receive.

Brainstorm and list all the value you get in your current role. Think about money, benefits, flexibility, access to resources, learning opportunities, and beyond. It's important to avoid tunnel vision and keep sight of how your role brings you value. Everything is a trade-off. Think about whether you're being myopic in evaluating different values you get from work; this can often lead to regretable career decisions.

15 MINUTES

Target an award.

What awards or ranking could you go after in your area? Think inside of your organization or in the greater business community. Pick one and download the application. What are they looking for? Take a few minutes and evaluate your achievements based on the criteria. It would be lovely to be "award-winning," but often there's tremendous value in going through the application process. It's a great way to *force* yourself to look at your successes from an outside perspective. That perspective can be very useful to remind yourself, and your team, just what you're contributing.

12

CAREER PLANNING

How many times does someone ask in an interview *where do you see yourself in five*

years? Who can answer that, these days? The world of work is changing so fast I'm not sure anyone can plan too much detail or with any real accuracy. What we can do is be intentional and mindful of the trends in our industry. You can set yourself up for future success.

Think about career planning in terms of making sure you "dig the well before you're thirsty." Educate yourself on your options. Where does your current role lead within your organization? What internal politics or industry trends are most likely to affect what happens next? You are not merely subject to happenstance. You can absolutely create oceans of future opportunities that in no way can be predicted from where you sit today. Take the time to steer your career.

5 MINUTES

Ask for an introduction to the manager.

Identify someone who knows the manager of a department where you might want to work. Ask for an introduction to the manager, so they know who you are and that you're interested. The next time they have an opening, they might think of you.

5 MINUTES

Make an HR appointment.

Schedule a meeting with HR to ask how you should be preparing for the next steps in your career. Focus on how you want your career to grow and evolve; as opposed to why you are stretching out of your current role. Ask them if they will partner with you to make next steps happen.

ACTION

Who are two to three people, which have recently or will soon get promoted? How often do people get promoted in your company? What makes them successful? What do they have in common? How are they different? What can you learn from their success?

10 MINUTES

Shadow your dream job.

Who has the job title you want next? Write an email and ask if you can shadow them in their job for a half day. What do they wish they knew before they took this job? Ask for a conversation, and learn how they spend their time every day. Nothing is worse than working hard to achieve a position, only to find out you don't like the actual work!

10 MINUTES

ACTION

Get online and look at recent headlines for your industry. Identify a trendy skill that looks like it will be important to learn for your future. What is one thing you can do to get access to that skill?

15 MINUTES

Target specific departments.

What departments might be of interest to you? Make a list of three things that are most interesting about each department. What three questions could you ask someone from each department that would best help you understand if there is a role that would be of interest to you?

ACTION

Name two to three job titles that may be likely next steps in your career. Go search for these titles on any job board and look at the requirements. Note the skills you do or don't have.

15 MINUTES

Invest in yourself.

What coaching, classes, or support do you personally want to invest in yourself, even if your company will not? Make a list and commit to one today. If you're not willing to invest in yourself, why should your employer invest in you?

15 MINUTES

Outline the value of your projects.

Craft an outline of the value of your projects. How are you saving money? Reducing cost? Improving efficiency? Reducing waste? How can you bring context to what you're working on? Size of project? Number of people? Budget? Scope? Number of countries? People need context to understand what you're bringing to the table.

CONCLUSION

You have the power.
You can change the
trajectory you're on just
by waking up. You don't

need another job, or a different boss, to get started. You can take small steps right where you are. Make this the perfect time to create **lots** of small moments, which will fuel you forward. Momentum is a powerful thing. Every action contained in this book is here to foster and grow your momentum.

You are unstoppable. Miraculous things are in front of you. All you have to do is wake up and smell the coffee.

Wishing you work happiness,

ABOUT THE AUTHOR

Jennifer Way is a national speaker, author, and consultant that connects attracting and growing top talent with personal career management. She is the founder of Way Solutions, a consulting firm that serves companies and individuals with specific retention and career strategies. Her clients, medium-sized businesses to Fortune 50, all believe that talent is a competitive advantage and strive to create greater work happiness for themselves and others. Jennifer's most proud of her individual clients who reframed the value they bring to their organizations to negotiate promotions, salary increases, and greater visibility and rewards for themselves.

Jennifer frequently speaks, blogs, and consults on behalf of CareerBuilder. She authored several of their learning series curriculums and often facilitates workshops on their behalf. Prior to her current company, she served as a Director of Recruiting for marchFIRST, National Recruiting Project Manager for KPMG, and led field recruiting for Dollar General Corporation.

Jennifer is living the good life in Nashville, TN with her man and the sweetest pup there ever was.